TOUCH
THE
SKY

You can do whatever you set your mind to—all it takes
is guts and passion. Regardless of where you come from,
what you have or what you don't have, you too can achieve
your dream. If I can do it, so can you! You too can dare to
DREAM, LIVE, FLY!

Barrington Irving

Photographs © 2012: Addictive Simulations/www.addictive.it: 32; age fotostock: 88 (JTP Photo
Communications Inc.), 76 top (Duncan Maxwell/Robert Harding Picture Library); Alamy
Images: 76 bottom (Jon Bower Hong Kong), 79 (Ernest Manewal/Alaska Stock LLC), 77 (Photo
Japan); AlaskaStock.com: 78; AP Images: 83 (Bikas Das), 102, 103, 105 (Alan Diaz); Courtesy
of Barrington Irving Sr.: 19; Getty Images: 62 (De Agostini), 80 (Mathias Kniepeiss), 54, 58, 59
(Joe Raedle), 16 (Robert Sullivan/AFP); iStockphoto/Hao Liang: 72; Jon Ross Photography:
back cover, cover background, cover foreground, 2, 15, 26, 42, 57; Courtesy of Juan Rivera: 10,
46, 47, 51, 53, 64, 66, 69, 71, 73, 75, 87, 93; Landov, LLC/Sarah Dussault/MCT: 34; NASA/
NASA's Earth Observatory: 6, 7; NEWSCOM: 84 (Deshakalyan Chowdhury/AFP/Getty
Images), 24 (Jeff Etessam/Icon SMI); ShutterStock, Inc.: 94 (Condor 36), 74 top (Maksym
Gorpenyuk), 74 bottom (haider), 100 (A. Hornung), 29 (Carlos E. Santa Maria); Used Courtesy
of The Black Archives of Mid-America in Kansas City, Inc.: 38, 39.

Copyright © 2012 by Barrington Irving and Holly Peppe.
All rights reserved. Published by Scholastic Inc.
Printed in the U.S.A.

ISBN-13: 978-0-545-50101-9
ISBN-10: 0-545-50101-6

6 7 8 9 10   40   21 20 19 18 17 16 15

TOUCH THE SKY

My Solo Flight Around the World

Barrington Irving
and
Holly Peppe

SCHOLASTIC INC.
New York Toronto London Auckland
Sydney New Delhi Hong Kong

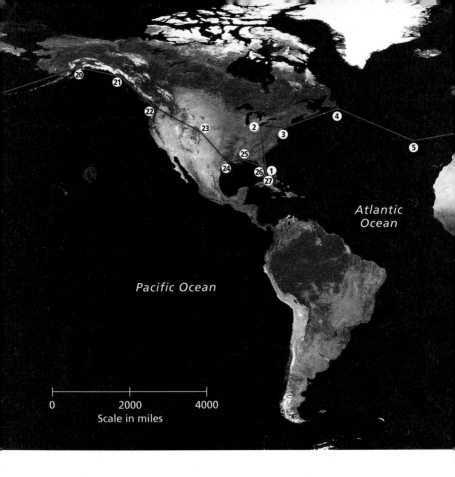

THE**FLIGHT**PATH

BARRINGTON IRVING BECAME THE YOUNGEST
PERSON—AND THE FIRST BLACK PILOT—
TO FLY SOLO AROUND THE WORLD.

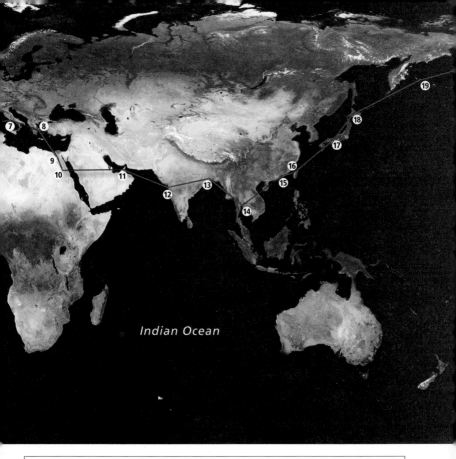

Indian Ocean

1 Miami, Florida	**10** Luxor, Egypt	**19** Shemya, Alaska
2 Cleveland, Ohio	**11** Dubai, UAE	**20** Anchorage, Alaska
3 Farmingdale, NY	**12** Mumbai, India	**21** Juneau, Alaska
4 St. John's, Canada	**13** Kolkata, India	**22** Seattle, Washington
5 Santa Maria, Azores	**14** Bangkok, Thailand	**23** Denver, Colorado
6 Madrid, Spain	**15** Hong Kong, China	**24** Houston, Texas
7 Rome, Italy	**16** Taipei, Taiwan	**25** Mobile, Alabama
8 Athens, Greece	**17** Nagoya, Japan	**26** Orlando, Florida
9 Cairo, Egypt	**18** Asahikawa, Japan	**27** Miami, Florida

Contents

EYE IN THE SKY High over the Atlantic, en route to the Azores islands, Irving took a moment to photograph the view from the cockpit of his plane.

CHAPTER 1

DON'T
PANIC

I'm all alone in a single-engine plane, high over the North Atlantic Ocean. Below there is nothing but the deep, dark sea. It will take me 12 hours to reach my next stop—the Azores, a chain of islands in the middle of the Atlantic Ocean. They're 1,500 miles away. If anything goes wrong, I'll have no place to land.

Just two weeks ago, I started off on the adventure of a lifetime: to fly solo around the world. I'm only 23 years old. If I make it, I'll be the youngest person—and the first black pilot—to accomplish the feat. (The youngest person before me was 34.) I've spent the last two years training, planning, and dreaming about this journey. Now I can only ask myself: what was I thinking?

COLD COMFORT

I squirm in my seat, trying to get comfortable. I love my plane, *Inspiration*, but it is no luxury airliner. An extra fuel tank takes up all the room in the cabin behind me. There is no way to get up and walk around. I'm strapped in, sweating in a wool-lined rubber survival suit. If I have to ditch the plane in the ocean, the suit will protect me from the cold until I can be rescued. It will also keep me afloat if I get separated from my life raft. That's crucial, since I never learned to swim! This thought gives me a moment of comic relief, but it doesn't last.

The raging sea below looks way too close. I am tempted to try to climb above the cloud layer to gain precious altitude. But if the clouds are thick, my wings could ice over before I break through.

And what if my one and only engine quits? I mentally recite the emergency procedures I learned in flight school. Reduce my airspeed so I can glide as long as possible, but not so much that I stall the wings and fall like a rock. Open my cockpit door and close the latch so the door won't get jammed on impact. Pull my emergency locator transmitter (ELT) and life raft up next to me. Try to land parallel to the waves.

DEAD AIR

Suddenly the loud whine coming from the engine changes pitch—higher, then lower. Don't panic, I tell myself. Analyze the problem. I calm myself down and realize it's just the shifting winds playing with the propeller.

Thoughts of my friends and family distract me for a while. I take a few bites of a banana and drink a little water.

GATHERING INSPIRATION Irving's single-engine plane, *Inspiration,* carried barely enough fuel to get him through the longest legs of his around-the-world journey. ▶

Just when it feels as though the flight is going smoothly again, my radio goes dead. I bark into the transmitter, "N731 Echo Alpha, transmission on 121.5—anyone on the frequency, please acknowledge!" There's nothing but dead air. "Please acknowledge!"

I am hundreds of miles from land, and I have
lost all communication with the world. No one can
warn me if a storm approaches. If I go down now, I
don't see how anyone could find me.

People all over the world know about my
flight—and yet I have never felt so alone.

SEA OF SUPPORT Fans of Barrington Irving hold up his picture at Opa-Locka Airport in Miami, Florida.

CHAPTER 2

GROWING
PAINS

The frigid North Atlantic is a long way from my first home—warm, sunny Jamaica. I was born in 1983 in Spanish Town, not far from Kingston, the capital of Jamaica.

Growing up, I was a curious kid. My mom says that I drove her crazy by asking a million questions: "How does the washing machine work?" "How many people did it take to build our house?" "Why is the sun so hot?" "How do birds fly?" Little did I know that someday *I* would be flying too.

Even back then, I was fascinated by technology. I spent a lot of time in my Uncle Jeff's garage, watching him fix cars. That's where I learned how a car engine works. I could picture all the parts moving together under the hood to make the car move. My parents couldn't afford to buy me toy cars, so I'd build my own. On Saturday mornings I ran door to door, collecting soda caps. I used them as wheels on little cars that I built from juice boxes.

AMERICAN DREAM

When I was six years old, my parents moved us to Florida. They thought they could make a better living in the United States and that my two-year-old brother, Ricardo, and I would get a better education. We'd all have a brighter future.

We settled in a tough section of Miami called Carol City, and it didn't seem promising at first.

JUNIOR MECHANIC Irving lived in Jamaica until he was six. As a kid he learned about car engines in his uncle's garage. ▶

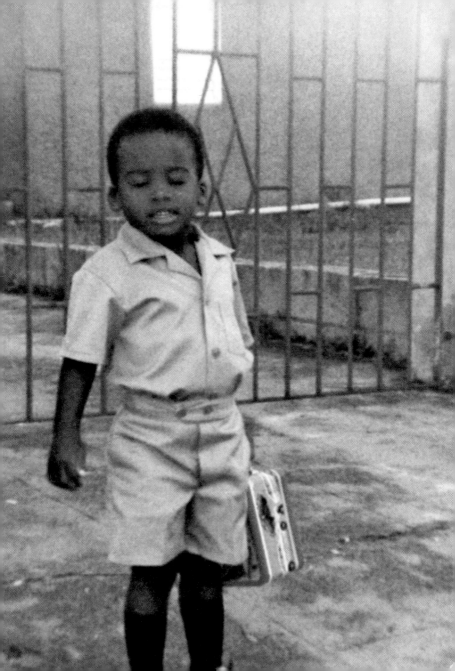

Loud music and the sound of sirens kept us awake at night. Sometimes we returned from evening church services to find police arresting someone at the house across the street. For a long time, my parents wouldn't let my brother or me leave our yard.

My parents worked hard to make ends meet. My mom, Clovalyn Irving, was a nurse's aide. My dad, Barrington James Irving, joined a construction crew. Soon after we moved to Miami, my dad earned a degree in religious studies. In 1996 he built a place to house our new family business, a Christian bookstore. My youngest brother, Christopher, was born that same year.

When we first arrived in Miami, I felt like an outsider. Kids picked on me nonstop in elementary school. They cracked jokes about my Jamaican accent. They teased me because I never seemed to have the right clothes, sneakers, or brand-name book bag.

AN OUTSIDER

I tried hard to fit in. I saved my lunch money and sold candy so I could buy a pair of Nikes. I would buy bags of candy for a dollar each and then sell pieces at a profit. I taped Airheads, Now and Laters, Snickers, and Kit Kats to my wrist. I'd hide them under my sleeve so I could sell them in class without getting busted by the teacher.

Toward the end of seventh grade, I saved up enough to buy my first pair of Nikes. But nothing changed. The other kids still ignored me.

One morning, while lacing up my new sneakers, I decided that if I couldn't fit in, I'd just do my own thing. After that I took special science classes with high school kids for two summers. I won awards in art and photography. Someday, I told myself, I'm going to do something great, something that will make the other kids wish they'd given me a chance.

A TICKET OUT

High school gave me even more motivation to find a way out of the hood. I went to Miami Northwestern, which is in Liberty City, about eight miles from my home. Liberty City was even rougher than Carol City. Some girls hid razor blades in their mouths in case they felt like starting a fight. I knew one guy who decided to rob a chain of auto parts stores. One night the police shot him in the chest seven times. He survived, but he was sent to jail.

Seeing all that violence made me realize that I had to get out of there. A friend of mine gave me some advice. The best way out, he told me, was football. Miami Northwestern's team was ranked third in the entire nation. If I made the team and played well, I had a chance of getting a scholarship to college. Who knows, I might even make it to the National Football League.

I tried out for the team my freshman year and made varsity. I played center for a while and then switched to fullback. I worked out in the gym to get stronger and faster. My coach and my teammates liked my positive attitude. I was willing to put it all on the line for the team.

Being good at football gave me a new feeling of confidence. I had always been shy around girls, but now *they* were trying to get *my* attention. The vibe in my neighborhood changed too. Some of the toughest guys started to respect me as one of the high school's rising stars. "Yo B!" they'd call out on the street. "What's up?" I'd wave back with a smile, "Not much!"

SURPRISE ENCOUNTER

At that point in my life I was busier than ever. Almost every day after school I had football practice. On weekends I bagged groceries at a local supermarket. I worked in my parents' bookstore

whenever I had time. It was during my hours at the bookstore that I learned how to run a business.

Life was hectic, but I had a goal. I wanted a career in football—that is, until one day in September 1999.

I was working in the bookstore when a man walked in who stood out from the usual neighborhood crowd. He wore a navy blue uniform with four gold stripes on his sleeve, the uniform of a United Airlines captain. I couldn't help but stare. It was the first time I had ever seen a black pilot.

Little did I know at the time how that one encounter would change my life.

◀ **EXIT STRATEGY** Irving hoped that football would be his ticket to college. His high school, Miami Northwestern, was a football powerhouse. During his four years there, 23 players earned college scholarships, and three went on to play in the NFL.

MENTOR Captain Gary Robinson (right) introduced Irving to aviation. Robinson says Irving was "a young man who needed someone to say 'you can do it.'"

CHAPTER 3

TAKING
FLIGHT

The pilot who walked into my parents' store that day introduced himself as Captain Gary Robinson. We talked a little. Then he asked me a simple question that would eventually shape my future: "Have you ever thought of becoming a pilot?"

The idea had never crossed my mind. "I don't think I'm smart enough," I blurted out. Then I asked, "Do you make good money as a pilot?"

Captain Robinson said he made $117 an hour, which definitely got my attention. But he pointed out that money wasn't everything. "You need to have a passion for what you do," he said.

"But you have to be smart like a rocket scientist to be a pilot, right?" I asked.

Captain Robinson laughed and shook his head. Then he invited me to come see the jet he flew.

SNEAK PREVIEW

The very next day, Captain Robinson gave me a ride to the airport. He flashed his badge and we passed through security. At the end of a tunnel, we stepped onto the tarmac and stood in front of a gigantic Boeing 777. Captain Robinson led me into the cockpit, where I was surrounded by gauges, buttons, and switches. My heart started to race. "Man!" I said. "If only I could learn to fly!"

FLYING DREAMS Irving decided he wanted to fly the moment he saw the complex controls inside the cockpit of a Boeing 777. ▶

"You can do whatever you want, son, if you want it badly enough," Captain Robinson said.

I decided that I wanted it—badly. I couldn't afford to buy materials about aviation, so I had to be creative. I scoured the library for books and videos on the subject. I called aircraft manufacturers and tried to sound like a prospective buyer so they would send me brochures. Instead of taking flight lessons for $110 an hour, I bought flight simulator software for $40 and downloaded it onto my parents' computer in the store. Now I could practice "taking off" and "landing"—without leaving work.

AIRBORNE

When I turned 16, Captain Robinson gave me the best birthday gift ever. He paid an instructor to take me up in a small plane. It was a windy day, and the plane bucked and bounced in the air. At first the turbulence scared me to death. But as the pilot banked high over the city, I saw parts of Miami that I had never seen before. I saw the wide blue ocean stretching to the horizon. My fear turned to joy, and I didn't want the flight to end.

The feeling I had that day has returned to me countless times since my first flight. Flying makes you feel so big and yet so small. You're a giant because you're on top of the world and everything below looks miniature. Yet you feel totally vulnerable because you're flying in a big empty space, surrounded by the heavens. Flying empowers you and humbles you at the same time.

By the time we landed, I was more determined than ever to become a pilot. I met a man who offered to take me flying in exchange for washing his small Cessna airplane. To earn money for more flight lessons, I cleaned swimming pools, in addition to working at the supermarket and the bookstore.

Then came my senior year—the pinnacle of my high school football career. My teammates and I were hoping that all our hours in the weight room

and on the practice field would pay off and that we'd be offered college scholarships. In the end I received not one but several offers to play football in college.

I turned them all down. I had a different dream: I wanted to get my pilot's license and go to college to study aviation.

Everyone thought I was crazy. My teammates and my coaches told me that I had just turned down the chance of a lifetime. My parents wondered how I was going to pay for college. I just had a gut feeling that I could make it work.

◀ **VIRTUAL PILOT** Irving bought flight simulation software to learn about flying. This program re-creates the experience of landing in thousands of real-life airports.

HIGHER LEARNING In 2003 Barrington Irving started classes at Florida Memorial University. He earned a full scholarship to attend the four-year college.

CHAPTER 4

GETTING OFF THE **GROUND**

In the fall of 2002, while my old teammates went off to college, I stayed home to become a pilot. I took classes at a community college. I put every cent I could into flight lessons. And at the age of 19, I earned my first pilot's license.

That was just the first step. Now I could fly small planes on my own, but I wanted to be a commercial pilot like Captain Robinson. I also wanted a degree in aeronautics so I could understand the science of flight.

While I pursued my degree at the community college, I spent as much time around pilots as I could. Whenever a group of pilots held an event in the Miami area, I volunteered to help.

COLLEGE SCHOLARSHIP

At the end of 2002 I volunteered at a party for the Tuskegee Airmen. The Tuskegee Airmen were the first black pilots in the U.S. military. They had trained in Tuskegee, Alabama, and fought together during World War II. They still have reunions across the country.

While I was stacking chairs at the party, I was approached by the aviation director at Florida Memorial University. FMU is a historically black college in Miami. The director had heard about me, and he offered me a chance to apply for a scholarship. If I was accepted, FMU and the U.S. Air Force would cover the cost of my tuition *and* my flight training courses.

Nine months later, I started at FMU with a full scholarship—and a full schedule. I spent every spare minute studying. I read about airflow, engine technology, weather patterns, and more. I trained with the air force, took flight lessons, and held a part-time job. I had no time to myself.

PAY IT FORWARD

Still, I kept thinking about something Captain Robinson had said to me: "I helped you. Make sure you help someone else." I thought back to my childhood in Carol City. I was lucky to have supportive parents and a great mentor like Captain Robinson. What if I shared my passion for flying with other young kids? Maybe I could get them hooked on a dream like mine.

I started talking to groups of kids in churches, schools, and community centers all over South Florida. Many of these kids were stuck in the cycle of poverty, crime, and violence that I had witnessed in high school. I remember meeting one

WAR HEROES Thirteen Tuskegee Airmen pose for a photo in 1943, the same year their fighter group went to Europe to fight in World War II. The group flew more than 1,500 combat missions during the war.

boy who had been left alone to care for his younger siblings. He had been breaking into homes and selling what he stole to buy food for his family.

I wanted to help kids like him see that they could make better lives for themselves. But talking wasn't enough. I needed to do something big to inspire them. I thought about flying around the state of Florida. That wasn't cool enough. What about flying to the capitals of all 50 states? Still not that thrilling.

SOMETHING SPECTACULAR

Finally it struck me: What if I flew around the world? I would prove that a young guy from a poor neighborhood could do something spectacular all on his own.

At first I only told a few people about my idea. My dad was surprised, but he supported me from the start. My mom didn't take me seriously until she saw a clip about me on the news. Then she got worried.

Captain Robinson seemed to like my idea of flying around the world. He said he'd be happy to help raise the money for plane tickets. I corrected him and explained that *I'd* be the pilot, circling the world on my own.

He looked at me with surprise, the full weight of the idea shocking him. "You'd be the *pilot*?!" he exclaimed.

PUTTING IT TOGETHER Irving couldn't afford to buy a plane, so he tried to convince companies to donate airplane parts. It was a tough process. "I got tons of rejection letters," he says.

CHAPTER 5

COUNTING
DOWN

The first thing you need if you're going to fly around the world is an airplane. Since a single-engine plane costs about $650,000, I couldn't afford one. But somehow, I had to find wings.

My first plan was to convince an aircraft manufacturer to supply a plane in exchange for the publicity that would come from my flight. That's where Fabio Alexander, an executive in the aviation business and one of my mentors, stepped in. He paid my way to go to aviation trade shows, where the latest airplanes and equipment are on display. Dressed in a suit and tie, I wore out my one good pair of shoes walking the length of the giant exhibition halls. But the answer was always the same. No one had an airplane for a 21-year-old.

My next plan came to me in a flash. I couldn't get a whole plane, but maybe I could get the parts, one by one. Then I would ask a manufacturer to assemble the plane for me.

PIECE BY PIECE

I went for the biggest part first—the engine. Letters hadn't gotten me anywhere, so I decided to make my request in person.

In the fall of 2005, I rented a car and made the 12-hour drive to Mobile, Alabama, home of Continental Motors. I didn't have money for a hotel, so I slept in the car. In the morning I put on my suit and tie and walked into the Continental headquarters. A representative, who assumed I was a potential buyer, gave me a tour of the plant.

Then I asked to meet the company president, Brian Lewis. He wasn't expecting me, but I told his secretary I would wait.

Two hours later I was called into his office. "You've got five minutes. Shoot!" Mr. Lewis said. I knew I had only one chance. I told him my life story in a few sentences. Then I explained my goal of circling the world to inspire other young people. I asked whether he would donate an airplane engine.

Mr. Lewis listened carefully but showed no expression. All he said afterward was, "Thank you, Mr. Irving."

I drove back home with no idea what to expect. A few weeks later, I got a phone call. The $83,000 engine was mine!

Once I had the engine, I made the rounds at the aviation shows again. This time the effort paid off. Many people felt that if Continental had given me an engine, my project must be worthwhile. Before I wore through another pair of shoes, I had been promised all the parts that I needed.

LOOKING FOR
INSPIRATION

Irving's plane was built with $300,000 in donated materials and services. Here's a partial list.

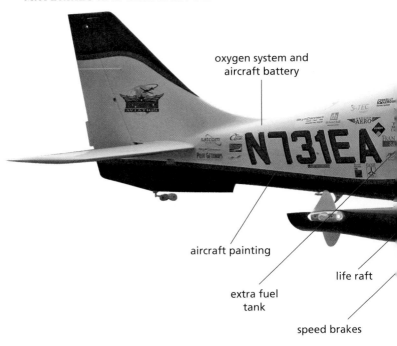

oxygen system and
aircraft battery

aircraft painting

life raft

extra fuel
tank

speed brakes

Plus . . .
- general support and flight training
- flight simulator tracking
- flight planning
- communication satellite technology

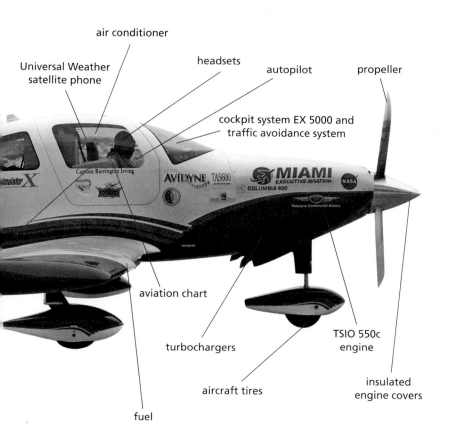

air conditioner

Universal Weather
satellite phone

headsets

autopilot

propeller

cockpit system EX 5000 and
traffic avoidance system

Captain Barrington Irving

aviation chart

turbochargers

TSIO 550c
engine

aircraft tires

insulated
engine covers

fuel

Columbia Aircraft offered to build the plane for $350,000, about half the cost of starting from scratch. It would take me years to pay off the balance, but I was on my way.

IN TRAINING

With the plane taken care of, I got serious about planning and training. I started lifting weights to get my body in shape for long flights. It may seem strange, but sitting in one place for hours on end takes strength and stamina.

I also practiced my piloting skills. I flew over mountains. I flew through rain and snow. To get used to crossing large bodies of water, I flew to Jamaica. Fabio Alexander sponsored me to fly to Colombia.

Juan Rivera, a good friend of mine, sometimes joined me on my practice flights. Juan and I had met in photography class in high school. We also played football together. Juan was pursuing a career in film. I told him about my around-the-world adventure, and we hatched a plan: Juan would follow me on commercial flights and film me in different countries. Then he would make a documentary of my trip.

A public relations professional named Holly Peppe helped me figure out other ways to tell the world about my voyage. She got the word out to newspapers and magazines. She also set up a website where kids could follow the flight.

To plan my route, I called Keith Foreman at Universal Weather and Aviation in Houston, Texas. Keith's team of 15 flight planners and weather specialists helped design a flight plan that would take me to 25 cities around the world.

Keith helped me get permits to fly over the countries I needed to cross. Not every country is friendly with the United States, and I didn't want to get shot down for flying into a hostile nation's airspace. He also found me a local handler for each stop. The handlers would reserve hotel rooms, set up ground transportation, and get me legal permission to enter the country.

Keith would have another role to play once I was airborne—a role that could mean life or death for me. He would tell me if raging storms, high winds, thick fog, or other wild weather lay ahead. I had no weather radar on board *Inspiration*, so I'd have to rely on a radio and a satellite phone for vital updates from Keith.

NO TURNING BACK

As my takeoff neared, the dangers of the trip began to sink in. *Inspiration* had few of the safety features that large jetliners have.

First, my plane didn't have de-icing equipment to break ice off the wings in freezing weather. If the wings iced over, the added bulk could disrupt the airflow and send me hurtling to the ground.

Inspiration also had a limited fuel supply. Even with an extra tank, the plane carried barely enough

WING AND A PRAYER Barrington Irving stands next to *Inspiration*, the single-engine plane he was relying on to carry him around the world. ▶

fuel to get me through the longest flights. During the ocean crossings, I'd be flying for hours over open seas. If a sudden storm broke out, I would have nowhere to land. And I might not have enough fuel to detour around the bad weather.

What's more, my plane didn't have a pressurized cabin. That could make it difficult for me to stay alert at high altitudes. As I climbed, the air pressure would drop and there would be less oxygen for me to breathe. At altitudes above 12,500 feet, I would need to breathe oxygen from a tank. Low oxygen levels make people dizzy and sick, and I wouldn't have a co-pilot to take over if I needed to rest.

Worries swirled inside my head like storm clouds. Was I really ready for this trip? I'd be traveling 30,000 miles, around the world, on my own.

But there was no turning back.

TRAINING TIME Irving practiced water rescues in an indoor tank. The inflatable life vest he's wearing here was crucial because he didn't know how to swim. ▶

GOOD-BYE AND GOOD LUCK Thousands of fans gathered at Opa-Locka Airport in Miami to watch Irving take off. The young men in red ties are members of a mentoring club that Irving belonged to in high school.

CHAPTER 6

TAKEOFF

On March 23, 2007, the scene at Miami's
Opa-Locka Airport was just amazing. More than
5,000 people showed up to see me off. There
were students, teachers, sponsors, church groups,
politicians, Tuskegee Airmen, U.S. Air Force cadets,
cheerleaders, and a marching band from my high
school. Children waved U.S. and Jamaican flags.

People cheered wildly when I stepped out to
greet the crowd. I stood at a podium and thanked
everyone who had supported me. "If you have a

SMALL PIECE OF THE SKY Irving finally gets airborne over Miami after four years of planning. His plane was only 25 feet long and nine feet high, with a wingspan of 36 feet. ▶

dream, you must put your energy toward making it happen," I said. "Don't let anyone tell you your dream isn't good enough." I could hear my mother sobbing behind me.

When I finished speaking, the crowd erupted in applause. Captain Robinson walked my family and

me out to the plane. My father held onto me for a
long moment. My mother could barely speak. "I
won't cry," she said as she continued to weep.

I climbed into *Inspiration*, and a moment later I
was airborne. I felt like I had touched the sky at last.

AIR SUPPORT More than 5,000 people, most of them kids, cheered for Irving as he took off from Miami on March 23, 2007.

FIRST FLIGHTS

The first part of my flight took me to Cleveland and then to New York City. In both cities I talked to reporters and to student groups. In New York I appeared on several morning news programs. People started to recognize me on the street. "Aren't you the pilot who's flying around the world?" they'd ask. "Weren't you on TV?"

"Hey, B," Juan teased, "you haven't even left the States and you're already a star."

I left New York City, headed for St. John's, Canada. I arrived just ahead of a snowstorm, so there I stayed, grounded by the weather.

I finally took off again on April 7, a week and a half behind schedule. That's how I ended up where this story began: midair over the North Atlantic Ocean. It was my first big test, and I was in trouble. When my communication system went dead, I struggled to stay calm. By that time I had been in the air for almost seven hours. I couldn't think straight anymore. I desperately wanted to get

TRAVELING**LIGHT**

To keep his flying weight low, Irving had to limit what he brought aboard to a few essentials. Here's his packing list.

- aviation charts and maps
- waterproof survival suit
- flight suit
- clothes (jeans and T-shirts, button-down dress shirt)
- boots
- tool kit
- portable oxygen tank
- Bible
- extra engine oil
- satellite phone
- high-energy drinks
- bottled water
- candy bars
- first-aid kit
- inflatable life raft
- handheld video camera

out of the plane. My heart began to race faster than the engine. My suit filled with sweat even though it was freezing inside the plane.

HELPING HANDS

Thankfully, my radio crackled back to life. The plane started flying smoothly again. I thought of my family. My two younger brothers, Ricardo and Christopher, were probably at home tracking my

flight on the web. In the last hour of the flight, with a tailwind speeding *Inspiration* along, I recalled the uplifting messages posted on my website. Encouraged, I flew on. At last I saw the cluster of small islands where I would be landing. I had arrived at the Azores.

When I finally touched down after 12 hours in the air, I didn't have the strength to climb out of the plane. I spent 30 minutes trying to stretch out my cramped legs. Finally I crawled out on my elbows onto the wing and lowered myself onto the tarmac. A member of the ground crew reached out to help me. He said something in Portuguese. I didn't speak his language, so I replied with the only Spanish words I knew: *"Muchas gracias."*

◀ **SOLID GROUND** For the first major stage of his journey, Irving flew 1,500 miles across the Atlantic Ocean. He landed in the Azores islands (left), about 800 miles off the coast of Portugal.

SPANISH HOLIDAY Juan Rivera took this photo in downtown Madrid. Rivera and Irving spent two days exploring the historic Spanish capital.

CHAPTER 7

WORLD
TOUR

After I left the Azores, my route took me through three of Europe's most majestic cities: Madrid, Spain; Rome, Italy; and Athens, Greece.

Despite some treacherous weather, I was flying with new confidence. The ordeal over the North Atlantic had boosted my morale. I had never flown that long in a single stretch. It was the first test of all my planning and training. And even though I came close to giving up, I had found a way to make it through. If I could survive that, I could survive anything, I thought.

While my feet were on solid ground, I had a great time in Europe. I had never been overseas before, and I was amazed by the graceful architecture and the centuries of history built into everything we saw. Juan and I wandered the cobblestone streets of Rome, wondering what life was like before automobiles and airplanes. We toured the Roman Colosseum, where gladiators once battled lions and alligators. We saw a marble stadium in Athens that hosted athletic events more than 2,000 years ago.

GROUNDED IN GREECE

When it came time to leave for the Middle East, the weather got in the way once again. I was headed for Egypt, but sandstorms in the Egyptian desert blocked my route. I had to sit in my hotel in Athens and wait for the weather to clear.

◀ **LIVING HISTORY** Irving stands inside the Colosseum in Rome. Some 2,000 years ago, when the Colosseum was built, as many as 55,000 spectators would gather there to watch enslaved people battle wild animals.

OFFICIAL PHOTOGRAPHER Juan Rivera, a friend from high school, followed Irving around the world to document the trip. Rivera took many of the photos in this book. ▶

Frustration began to set in. It was the middle of April, and I was weeks behind schedule. The original plan had me in India already, ahead of monsoon season. The monsoons would soon bring hurricane-force winds and heavy rains to South Asia. And here I was still stuck in Europe.

To lift my spirits, I called Captain Robinson, Fabio, Holly, and my parents. Then I checked my website and read letters posted by kids who were following my progress. One of them really made me smile. "Dear Barrington," it read. "While you are in Mumbai, India, try catching some snakes. Be careful going over wars. Bring back a baby snake from Mumbai to my school."

WORLD OF WONDERS

After three days, I was able to take off for Cairo, Egypt. The very next day, I found myself trotting through the desert on a horse. The Great Pyramid of Khufu, one of the largest structures ever built, towered 450 feet over my head. At least 10,000 people had labored for more than 20 years to build it. Somehow they transported and stacked two million stone blocks that weighed an average of three tons each. And they did it without the help of motorized vehicles.

Juan had met me in Cairo. He rode beside me on a camel, recording it all on his video camera.

"Man," I said to him. "Can you believe we made it this far?"

FIT FOR A KING Irving poses in front of the Great Pyramid, 6,500 miles from his starting point in Miami. The pyramid was built to house the body of Pharaoh Khufu. It stands 450 feet high and was built more than 4,500 years ago. ▶

AROUND THE WORLD
IN 97 DAYS

HERE ARE SOME OF THE STOPS BARRINGTON IRVING
MADE DURING HIS RECORD-SETTING JOURNEY.

ROME, ITALY Juan and I visited the Colosseum (below), the ancient amphitheater where gladiators fought lions, crocodiles, monkeys, cheetahs—and each other. We also stopped at the Trevi fountain. Legend says that people who toss coins into the fountain will return to Rome. Let's hope so! And Italian gelato? Best ice cream ever! We stopped to have some at least eight or nine times. ▼

▲ **ATHENS, GREECE** This is the Panathenaic
stadium, which was built around 330 BCE to host
athletic events. It was made completely of marble
and had more than 50,000 seats. The stadium was
restored at the end of the 19th century for the
first modern Olympic Games in 1896.

▲ **CAIRO, EGYPT** Juan and I visited the Sphinx and the famous pyramids, which are the tombs of the ancient Egyptian kings. The Great Pyramid of Khufu (behind the Sphinx) is still one of the most massive buildings on earth and the only one of the Seven Wonders of the Ancient World that is still standing.

◀ **DUBAI, UNITED ARAB EMIRATES** The skyline of Dubai looks like New York City rising out of a desert. We were treated to a wild jeep ride up and down the sand dunes. We also visited malls that were fancier than any malls back home. There was even an indoor ski resort the size of three football fields! Skiers rented skis, boots, and even hats, scarves, and gloves. The temperature outside reaches 120°F in summer, but they keep the resort cooled to a chilly 32°F.

▲ **MUMBAI, INDIA** On the runway, I got a rare glimpse of a huge airliner, an Airbus A380, about to do a test flight. This plane would soon be the largest civilian aircraft in the sky. The silhouette under the tail of the Airbus shows how small my plane is in comparison!

▲ **KOLKATA, INDIA** After Mumbai, I flew to Kolkata, a city on India's eastern border. I saw many corporate jets at the airport, a sign of India's thriving aviation industry. But there seemed to be a very sharp division between rich and poor in Kolkata.

▲ **TOKYO, JAPAN** Juan and I rode the *Shinkansen*, Japan's extra-fast bullet train. It looked like an airplane without wings. The train rocketed down the track at 200 mph! I also got a taste of home. We learned from the Jamaican ambassador about examples of Jamaican culture right there in Japan.

◀ **HONG KONG, CHINA** After flying over 4,000-foot mountains, I started to feel like I'd flown this route before. And I had . . . sitting in front of the computer at my parents' bookstore! My flight simulator software had included a landing in Hong Kong. The only thing missing from the program was the weather and other planes landing at the same time. Once we got settled, Juan and I took a tram ride up to Victoria Peak, a 1,500-foot mountaintop that gave us a bird's eye view of the city.

SHEMYA, ALASKA The winds on this tiny island can reach 120 mph. That's hurricane speed. Everyone carries handheld radios when they walk outside in case they're about to be blown off the island. People are advised to walk in groups, never alone. The fog was so thick I couldn't see my hands in front of my face.

PIT**STOP**

AT 8,000 FEET, TAKING CARE OF BASICS WASN'T EASY.

On most transcontinental flights, passengers have flight attendants serving them meals and drinks. All I had were some candy bars, bananas, water, and energy drinks. Usually I fasted while I was in the air, sometimes for ten hours straight. Food was the last thing on my mind while trying to keep the plane airborne. I lost 30 pounds during three months of travel.

I also went to the bathroom sparingly. I had a tube to pee into, but that required acrobatics in a bulky flight suit. Even the slightest movements made my plane tilt or shake. To keep myself flying level, I usually just waited until I was safely on the ground.

ANCHORAGE TO JUNEAU, ALASKA This was the most beautiful part of the trip. I flew over volcanoes, a stunning coastline, and snowy mountains. ▼

FROZEN OASIS A snowboarder rides on a ski lift in Ski Dubai, the world's largest indoor ski resort. Dubai is also home to the world's tallest building—the Burj Khalifa. The world's largest airport and the world's largest arch bridge are also planned for the city.

CHAPTER 8

SAND AND
STORMS

I left Egypt on April 22 and flew across the
Persian Gulf to Dubai, one of the United Arab
Emirates. Dubai was a magical place, one of the
wealthiest cities in the world. I stayed in a hotel
that looked like a palace, went four-wheeling in the
desert, and visited a ski resort located inside a mall.

But while I was there, my luck took a turn
for the worse. During a routine inspection, we
discovered that *Inspiration* needed a new battery. It
was Wednesday, April 25, and the battery wouldn't

arrive until Monday. On Sunday we found that sand had damaged a part of the brakes. That took another two days to fix.

I finally got *Inspiration* running safely and made the flight to India. By then it was May 10. My original flight plan had me finishing the entire voyage by this time. But I wasn't even halfway through my route. Now I was stuck in Kolkata, India, with the monsoon season in full swing. A storm hovered over the Bay of Bengal, blocking my route to Thailand.

MONSOON**SEASON**

THESE STORMS CAN DO A LOT OF DAMAGE.

Monsoons are strong, seasonal winds that bring wet and dry seasons to various parts of the world. In India, summer monsoons bring the drenching rain that farmers need for their crops.

India's monsoon season typically starts in June. Warm, moist air rushes in from the sea, packing rain-filled clouds that soak the country throughout the summer. Monsoon winds can reach hurricane speeds, causing havoc for people living in India—and for pilots flying overhead!

MONSOON SEASON Monsoon clouds appear over Kolkata, India.

MONSOON MADNESS People travel along a flooded street in Kolkata, India, in June 2007, just after Irving was there. The city was hit by an especially severe monsoon season that year.

That wasn't even the worst of it. I had another long ocean crossing to make before I returned to the U.S. mainland. That flight would take me from Japan to Shemya, Alaska, a remote island in the frigid North Pacific. The U.S. Air Force has an aircraft refueling station there. But from late June through September, dense fog seals off Shemya from the rest of the world. If I didn't make it to Shemya by mid-June, I could be stuck for months.

All my plans seemed to be breaking down. I wanted to forget about the weather, jump into the cockpit, and fly. But I had to be patient. My life depended on it.

NOT A DAY TO DIE

On Wednesday, May 16, Keith and my friends at Universal thought they saw a break in the storms. I rushed to the airport and flew from Kolkata to Bangkok, Thailand. I landed safely and went straight to my hotel for a few hours of sleep.

By early morning I was back at the airport. I had a 1,200-mile flight to Hong Kong, China, ahead of me. The weather was closing in, and I had to get airborne fast or I wouldn't make it.

Somewhere over Vietnam, the monsoon caught up with me. I had flown through storms before, but nothing like this. At one point, as I flew over mountain terrain, a strong wind forced *Inspiration* to drop 10,000 feet in the blink of an eye. My head hit the roof of the cockpit. Then a rising column of air carried the plane straight back up. My life raft bounced around the cabin like a toy. "Not today," I prayed. "I will not die today."

Somehow my prayer was answered, and I touched down safely in Hong Kong. By the time I got out of the plane, I could barely keep my eyes open. Juan wanted to show me the city, but I made him take me to the hotel. I collapsed into bed and slept for 18 hours that night.

OUT ON THE TOWN After catching up on sleep, Irving explored Hong Kong at night. "Life in Hong Kong is fast-paced, and people and traffic are everywhere," he wrote in his blog. ▶

RURAL JAPAN Irving traveled to Nakashibetsu, a very small town in the northeastern tip of Japan, to make his flight across the Pacific Ocean.

CHAPTER 9

WAITING GAME

During the last week of May, I arrived in Japan.
And that's where I stayed, day after endless day,
waiting for the weather to clear over the North
Pacific.

For nine days I was stuck in Nakashibetsu, a
town in northern Japan. When I got to my hotel,
the desk clerk told me, "No TV in English." A
cold, dreary rain trapped me in my tiny room.
When I ventured outside, I saw nothing but
farmland for miles around. Juan had flown ahead

to Seattle, Washington, because we didn't have the money for him to follow me through this stage of my journey. I was alone, cut off from the rest of the world. I felt like an alien because I was the only black man in town.

Day after day, I called Keith for weather updates. Each day the answer was the same: "Not tomorrow or the next day. Let's hope for a window three or four days from now."

I began to sink into a deep depression. I knew it was just a matter of days before fog settled around the island of Shemya. Then it would be impossible to fly in or out.

What's more, my friend and fellow pilot Michael Atkins was waiting for me in Shemya. Months ago, we had planned for him to meet me there with fuel for my plane, which wasn't available on the island.

Every night as I tried to sleep, my mind strayed to the flight ahead. I'd have 1,760 miles to cover from Nakashibetsu to Shemya. The harrowing flight across the North Atlantic—my longest yet—

had been 170 miles shorter. And that was more than two months ago. Since then I had stopped working out and lost 15 pounds. Would I be strong enough to make it this time?

SECOND THOUGHTS

Even after flying through monsoons, electrical storms, and sandstorms, the challenges of the North Pacific frightened me. Temperatures would drop below freezing at dangerously low altitudes. The moisture in the clouds would ice my wings in a matter of seconds, forcing me to fly above the cloud cover. Winds could blow over 100 miles per hour, making it hard to maintain control of the plane. The waves below could swell to 60 or 70 feet. If I had to ditch the plane in the ocean there would be no chance of survival.

I wanted desperately to finish what I'd started. So many people were following my flight. I thought about the kids at home who dreamed about flying planes but weren't sure they had the skills or the resources to make it happen. I owed it to them to complete the trip. But at this point I really didn't think I was going to make it.

A FINAL GOOD-BYE

On June 10 I woke up at 5 A.M. and called Keith to check on the weather. A window of calm was opening over the North Pacific. Today would be my only chance.

I called my parents to say good-bye. I tried to sound confident over the phone. If I died, I didn't want my mother's last memory of me to be a voice filled with fear. I wanted her to remember my strength and determination.

On the tarmac, I saw my plane gleaming in the early light of daybreak. I kissed *Inspiration*'s nose for good luck. "It's me and you, baby," I said. "I'm taking you home now."

A VIEW FROM THE COCKPIT Irving took this photo as he was leaving Japan. ▶

BEAUTIFUL BUT DEADLY A towering cumulonimbus cloud looms in the sky, laden with moisture. Irving had to steer around clouds like these to keep ice from forming on his wings and knocking him out of the sky.

CHAPTER 10

THE LONGEST **DAY**

The islands of Japan disappeared behind me. For the next 1,500 miles, there would be no place to land.

Just minutes into the flight, powerful gusts of wind began to toy with my plane. I split my attention between my instruments and the cloud formations. At 7,000 feet, the moisture in those clouds would freeze on my wings. And the temperature was plunging fast. Before long the freezing level would drop to 2,000 feet. Alone over the vast Pacific Ocean, I needed to stay alert.

Suddenly a voice crackled on the radio: "Hey! What are you doing down there?"

Down there? The speaker was a pilot of a 747 jumbo jet. Jets fly way above the altitudes that my plane can manage. The pilot probably noticed me as a blip on his radar.

Voices from two other jets joined in: "What's happening down there? Who are you?"

I identified myself to the pilots and told them about my around-the-world flight. "You're a brave man to attempt such a journey in a single-engine aircraft," said one of the pilots. That brief comment gave me strength.

Then two other pilots advised me to turn back because there was bad weather ahead. I knew this was good advice, but I didn't have enough fuel to turn back. I had no choice but to keep going.

In a matter of minutes, all the jet pilots were far ahead of me.

I knew I'd need to draw on every ounce of strength I had to make it to Shemya. Even in my thermal suit I was chilled to the bone. The temperature outside the plane's thin hull dropped to -40°F. The turbulence became unbearable. I felt like I had climbed inside a saltshaker. The winds were raging between 70 and 110 miles per hour. At times I thought I was going to lose control of the plane. I'd be flying level when a harsh wind would push me on a sharp angle. Around me I saw swirling clouds. Below, the whitecaps of the Pacific Ocean seemed to be waiting for me.

INTO THE CLOUDS

Just an hour from Shemya, I encountered a wall of clouds that rose as high as the eye could see. My weather reports told me that there were massive ice-storm cells embedded within them. Would I have enough fuel to climb above the clouds? I wasn't sure, but I had to try. As I climbed above 12,000 feet I started to breathe bottled oxygen. I kept climbing, but the wall of clouds looked like it would never end. Gradually, my oxygen supply ran out. I started to feel light-headed and weak.

Finally, at 21,000 feet, I cleared the top of the cloud bank. Before me was a beautiful sight, a sea of white, fluffy clouds with the sun casting a golden glow over them. I stayed above the clouds as long as possible, even though my fingers started to turn blue from the lack of oxygen.

As I approached Shemya, I gritted my teeth and descended through a final blanket of clouds. Small drops of water on *Inspiration*'s wings froze into ice crystals. I tried to stay calm. I had gotten this far; I wasn't going to lose hope now.

At about 800 feet, I popped out the other side of the cloud bank. I saw the foggy island of Shemya below. After speeding through a dark and windy corridor of clouds, I touched down safely. I only had 20 minutes' worth of fuel left in my tank.

Taxiing down the runway, I felt like I was in shock. Michael Atkins and a small welcoming party held up a sign that said "WELCOME TO SHEMYA," with a photo of *Inspiration* beneath the words. I was touched by the welcome. Physically, though, I felt completely destroyed. I opened the aircraft door but had to spend 20 minutes contracting and relaxing my leg muscles before I could exit the aircraft. I was fatigued, and my body ached and cramped from turbulence and the lack of oxygen.

Walking slowly away from my plane, I saw a huge wall of gray fog approaching. "You arrived just in time," said Michael. "No way you could have flown through that."

AMERICA THE BEAUTIFUL Of all the landscapes Irving flew over, he thought Alaska's were the most striking.

CHAPTER 11

HOME SWEET **HOME**

After eight days in Shemya, hemmed in by fog and high winds, I flew to Anchorage, Alaska—mainland USA. When I touched down, I wanted to kiss the ground.

The next week was a homecoming tour for me. From Anchorage, I flew to Juneau, Seattle, Denver, Houston, and Mobile. I felt like a rock star. Fans greeted me at every stop and asked for my autograph. Keith and his team in Houston gave me a hero's welcome. We all breathed a sigh of relief.

Finally, on June 27, 2007, three months after my departure, I broke through the clouds one last time. I was six weeks behind schedule, but I had finally made it to Miami. I could see a crowd

WATER SALUTE Firefighters at Opa-Locka Airport welcome Irving home after his three-month-long flight around the world.

of people and TV cameras lining the runway. I rocked the plane back and forth in a "wing wave" greeting. When the wheels of *Inspiration* hit the runway, I officially became a record-setting pilot.

I climbed down from the wing and embraced my parents, my brothers, Captain Robinson, Fabio, Holly, Juan, and many others who had supported me from the start. I rested my forehead on *Inspiration*'s wing and bowed my head to give thanks for my safe return.

* * *

My trip around the world changed me forever. I had started out as an average kid who wanted to be somebody. I was lucky enough to meet Captain Robinson. He encouraged me to follow my dreams even though I didn't have any money and didn't think I was smart enough to learn to fly.

HOME AT LAST Irving is greeted by his parents and his two brothers. ▶

Now it was my turn to pass on some of that encouragement to other kids. After I completed my flight, it seemed like everyone wanted me to come and speak. I started a nonprofit organization called Experience Aviation, which runs after-school programs that introduce kids to careers in aviation and other science- and math-based fields.

In all the things I do, my message is the same: Regardless of where you come from, what you have or don't have, you too can achieve your dream. Believe in yourself. If I can do it, so can you.

A CONVERSATION WITH CO-AUTHOR HOLLY PEPPE

Q *When did you meet Barrington Irving?*

A I met Barrington in 2006, when he was planning his trip around the world. He wanted the world to know that he was undertaking the journey to show other young people that if he could achieve his dream, they could too. He asked me for assistance because I had experience with the international media. I had been public relations director for ORBIS, a medical organization that teaches eye surgery in developing countries inside a jet specially equipped as a hospital.

Q *As Irving's manager and publicist, what kind of work do you do for him?*

A I help Barrington make decisions that will help further his career. I also work closely with the companies that sponsor his visits to schools nationwide. During his around-the-world trip, I coordinated communications between him and his support team. In my role as publicist for the flight, I wrote press releases and text for his website. I also set up appearances for him on CNN, NBC's

Today Show, and other media outlets. His story was featured in thousands of print and online articles, on more than 400 radio shows, and in 900 TV segments, reaching more than two million people.

Q *What was the greatest challenge for you?*

A Those of us on Barrington's support team felt like we were traveling around the world with him. Because his journey took him through all 24 of the times zones in the world, it was often necessary to stay up through the night to follow his progress.

Q *Please describe your process for writing the book with Irving.*

A I recognized the richness of Barrington's story when I first heard him talk about his background as a young man whose mentor changed his life. Soon after, we talked about putting a book together. I was always jotting down notes from our conversations about the flight. Later I interviewed the people closest to him—his parents and brothers, Captain Robinson, and his best friend, Juan, to round out his life story. During the flight, Barrington wrote journal entries that he sent to me every few days to post on his website. I edited those entries and included them in the book. I also included comments from the many students, teachers, pilots, and others who sent Barrington messages online, cheering him on.

FOR FURTHER READING

Books

Airplane Flying Handbook, edited by the Federal Aviation Administration. (288 pages) *The official U.S. government guide to piloting aircraft*

The Airplane: How Ideas Gave Us Wings, Jay Spenser. (352 pages) *An explanation of every aspect of the development and evolution of airplanes*

Black Eagles: African Americans in Aviation, Jim Haskins. (208 pages) *African American achievements in aviation*

Flygirl, Sherri L. Smith. (288 pages) *A black teenager pretends she's white so that she can fly during World War II.*

Films and Videos

The Magic of Flight (1996). *This DVD explains what makes planes fly and shows stunts performed by the U.S. Navy's Blue Angels.*

One Six Right: The Romance of Flying (2005). *A documentary about one small airport in California*

The Tuskegee Airmen (1995) *A feature film about the historic flyers*

Websites

www.experienceaviation.org
This is Barrington Irving's site, and it includes information about his flight.

Barrington's Favorites

Private Pilot Manual, Jeppesen Sanderson

Stick and Rudder: An Explanation of the Art of Flying, Wolfgang Langewiesche

AOPA Flight Training Magazine and website:
http://flighttraining.aopa.org

GLOSSARY

altitude (AL-ti-tood) *noun* the distance above sea level or the surface of Earth

bullet train (BUL-it TRANE) *noun* another name for the *Shinkansen*, the network of high-speed passenger trains in Japan

frigid (FRIJ-id) *adjective* freezing cold

gladiator (GLAD-ee-ay-tur) *noun* in Ancient Rome, a person who was forced or chose to fight animals or other gladiators as a form of entertainment

harrowing (HA-row-ing) *adjective* extremely hard; unbearable

laden (LAYD-uhn) *adjective* carrying a lot of something

majestic (muh-JESS-tik) *adjective* very impressive, grand, and dignified

mentor (MEN-tor) *noun* a trusted teacher or guide

monsoon (mon-SOON) *noun* a seasonal shift in the wind patterns of a region

morale (muh-RAL) *noun* a person's mood or confidence level

tarmac (TAR-mak) *noun* an airport runway or taxiway

taxi (TAK-see) *verb* to drive a plane along the ground before taking off or after landing

tram (TRAM) *noun* a small train that runs on tracks through city streets

transmitter (transs-MIT-uhr) *noun* an electronic device that sends out radio signals

treacherous (TRECH-ur-uhss) *adjective* dangerous

turbulence (TUR-byuh-luhnss) *noun* irregular movement of air that causes a plane to shake

BIBLIOGRAPHY

"At 23, the Youngest Pilot to Solo the Planet," Vincent M. Mallozzi. *New York Times*, July 18, 2007.

"Back Talk with Barrington Irving," Sheiresa McRae. *Black Enterprise*, September 1, 2007.

"Barrington Irving Making History." *National Weekly*, March 27, 2007.

"Barrington Irving's Around-the-World Flight is Cause for Celebration," The Children's Trust. www.TheChildrensTrust.com. (including quote on page 26)

Barrington Irving's speech at Opa-Locka Airport. Miami, Florida, March 23, 2007.

"Cessna 150 Preflight," Ken Shuck. www.Cessna150.net.

"Experience Aviation," Barrington Irving. www.ExperienceAviation.org.

"Inspiration on the Wing: Around the World and Back with Barrington Irving," Clayton Moore. www.AirportJournals.com. (including quote on page 42)

"Our Boy," Ingrid Brown. *Jamaica Observer*, August 4, 2007.

"Pilot Shares Story of Success," Laurie D. Willis. *Salisbury Post*, November 6, 2010.

"Sweet Inspiration: Passing the Baton," Frances Fiorino. *Business Aviation Now*, April 17, 2007.

"Trailblazing Black Pilot Inspires Students at Astoria School," Nathan Duke. *New York Post*, January 20, 2010.

"Where in the World Is Barrington Irving?" Cnweeklynews.com. (including quote on page 87)

"Young Pilot Flies with 'Inspiration,'" Gordon Williams. *Jamaica Gleaner*, March 26, 2007.

ACKNOWLEDGEMENTS

I am grateful to the many companies and individuals that made this flight possible.

Thank you to my lead sponsors: Miami Executive Aviation, Universal Weather and Aviation, Microsoft Flight Simulator, Teledyne Continental Motors, Jeppesen, Avidyne, Chevron Global Aviation, Gill Battery, Goodyear, Hartzell, Kelly Aerospace, Light Speed, Oregon Aero, Precise Flight, Satcom, Scheme Designers, Seamech International, Inc., Start Pac, Sky Connect, S-Tec, Tanis Aircraft Services, and Winslow Life Raft.

I also want to thank the dedicated team who followed me every day of my 97-day flight, providing logistical, moral, and spiritual support: Captain Gary Robinson; Keith Foreman; Fabio Alexander; Holly Peppe; my parents, Barrington and Clovalyn Irving; and my brothers, Ricardo and Christopher. I'd also like to thank Juan Rivera for his friendship and commitment to the project; with unfailing enthusiasm and good humor, he followed me around the world, capturing my adventures in photos and video clips along the way. I'd also like to thank pilots Michael Atkins and Scot Evans, photographer Jon Ross, and project managers Myleen Arcia and Duane Lawrence for their support. I would also like to thank NASA for providing access to 87,000 students nationwide who tracked my flight as part of the NASA curriculum.

I am grateful for the thousands of students and others who followed my journey online, both in school and at home. Your many messages of encouragement throughout the trip fueled my determination to make it all the way around the globe.

—*Barrington Irving*

INDEX